'S

NEW BEGINNINGS

Finding God in the Unknown

Matthew A. Glover

*A ministry of the Diocese of Little Rock
in partnership with Liturgical Press*

Nihil obstat: Jerome Kodell, OSB, *Censor Librorum.*
Imprimatur: ✠ Anthony B. Taylor, Bishop of Little Rock, October 2, 2018.

Cover design by Ann Blattner. Cover photo: Getty Images. Used with permission.

Photos/illustrations: Pages 6, 13, 16, 19, 26, 29, 35, 37, Getty Images. Used with permission. Page 32, Clifford M. Yeary. Used with permission. Page 33, Lightstock. Used with permission.

ISBN: 978-0-8146-4418-8 (print); 978-0-8146-4443-0 (e-book)

Contents

Introduction

Alive in the Word brings you resources to deepen your understanding of Scripture, offer meaning for your life today, and help you to pray and act in response to God's word.

Use any volume of **Alive in the Word** in the way best suited to you.

- **For individual learning and reflection,** consider this an invitation to prayerfully journal in response to the questions you find along the way. And be prepared to move from head to heart and then to action.
- **For group learning and reflection,** arrange for three sessions where you will use the material provided as the basis for faith sharing and prayer. You may ask group members to read each chapter in advance and come prepared with questions answered. In this kind of session, plan to be together for about an hour. Or, if your group prefers, read and respond to the questions together without advance preparation. With this approach, it's helpful to plan on spending more time for each group session in order to adequately work through each of the chapters.

- **For a parish-wide event or use within a larger group,** provide each person with a copy of this volume, and allow time during the day for quiet reading, group discussion and prayer, and then a final commitment by each person to some simple action in response to what he or she learned.

This volume on the topic of new beginnings is one of several volumes that explore **Seasons of Our Lives**. While the Scriptures remain constant, we have the opportunity to find within them a fresh message as we go through life facing various challenges. Whether the circumstances in our lives change due to our own decisions or due to the natural process of aging and maturing, we bring with us the actual lived experiences of this world to our prayerful reading of the Bible. This series provides an opportunity to acknowledge our own circumstances and to find how God continues to work in us through changing times.

From Wilderness to Newness

Begin by quietly asking God to assist you in your prayer and study. Then read the three passages from Exodus below, each of which follows the Israelites in the journey through the wilderness.

Exodus 16:1-3
¹Having set out from Elim, the whole Israelite community came into the wilderness of Sin, which is between Elim and Sinai, on the fifteenth day of the second month after their departure from the land of Egypt. ²Here in the wilderness the whole Israelite community grumbled against Moses and Aaron. ³The Israelites said to them, "If only we had died at the LORD's hand in the land of Egypt, as we sat by our kettles of meat and ate our fill of bread! But you have led us into this wilderness to make this whole assembly die of famine!"

Exodus 17:1-3
¹From the wilderness of Sin the whole Israelite community journeyed by stages, as the LORD directed, and encamped at Rephidim.

But there was no water for the people to drink, ²and so they quarreled with Moses and said, "Give us water to drink." Moses replied to them, "Why do you quarrel with me? Why do you put the LORD to a test?" ³Here, then, in their thirst for water, the people grumbled against Moses, saying, "Why then did you bring us up out of Egypt? To have us die of thirst with our children and our livestock?"

Exodus 19:1-8

¹In the third month after the Israelites' departure from the land of Egypt, on the first day, they came to the wilderness of Sinai. ²After they made the journey from Rephidim and entered the wilderness of Sinai, they then pitched camp in the wilderness.

While Israel was encamped there in front of the mountain, ³Moses went up to the mountain of God. Then the LORD called to him from the mountain, saying: This is what you will say to the house of Jacob; tell the Israelites: ⁴You have seen how I treated the Egyptians and how I bore you up on eagles' wings and brought you to myself. ⁵Now, if you obey me completely and keep my covenant, you will be my treasured possession among all peoples, though all the earth is mine. ⁶You will be to me a kingdom of priests, a holy nation. That is what you must tell the Israelites." ⁷So Moses went and summoned the elders of the people. When he set before them all that the LORD had ordered him to tell them, ⁸all the people answered together, "Everything the LORD has said, we will do." Then Moses

brought back to the L<small>ORD</small> **the response of the people.**

Following a few moments of quiet reflection on the passages from Exodus, consider the background information provided in "Setting the Scenes."

Setting the Scenes

Not all new beginnings stem from, or result in, places of certainty. In fact, more often than not, new beginnings take shape in the midst of the unknown and can lead to even more unknowns than existed before. Along with the uncertainty of the unknown can come anxiety, stress, and fear. But in the arms of a providential God, even uncertain new beginnings can lead us ever more deeply into lasting relationship with God and with one another. Few people have known this truth more intimately than the Israelites in their great exodus from Egypt.

We all know the backstory described in Genesis 37–46: The Israelites landed in Egypt generations earlier when the family of Jacob moved there. Jacob's sons had sold their brother Joseph into slavery when they were younger, but Joseph worked his way into the pharaoh's service, becoming one of his most trusted advisors. In an ironic twist, Joseph's family migrated to Egypt seeking relief from famine in Canaan and were reunited and settled by their powerful brother. They grew and multiplied.

Over the course of time, a new pharaoh came to power who had no connection or loyalty to Joseph or his descendants, and this new pharaoh grew fearful of the Israelites' strength in numbers (Exod 1–2). So he enslaved them and treated them cruelly. Yahweh promised through Moses to deliver the Israelites from slavery (Exod 3), and after a series of plagues, the Israelites were set free—culminating in a dramatic escape from the Egyptians through the parted waters of the Red Sea (Exod 7–14).

But that was not the end of the Israelites' troubles. In fact, in some ways it was only the beginning. Having been liberated from enslavement in Egypt, the Israelites had to make a treacherous journey across a harsh desert climate to a promised land about which they knew very little. Although they'd been slaves in Egypt, at least there they had familiarity. Now, wandering in the desert, having gained their freedom, they lose any sense of familiarity and routine. Now they have to fend for themselves, make their own decisions, lead their own people—all with the providential guidance of Yahweh, whom they still continue to doubt, ignore, and even betray.

Although this adventure constitutes a new beginning for the Israelite people, it should come as no surprise that, given the circumstances, they are a bit wary of their newfound freedom. When things do not go exactly as anticipated in this new way of life, the Israelites begin to grumble and quarrel. The new beginning no doubt brought excitement, but it was the unknown that made them long for the good old days of Egypt.

> It was not until after Yahweh had responded to their grumbling that the people were properly disposed to enter into a new covenant with Yahweh.

The two most striking examples of this grumbling in the face of the unknown are found in the stories of the manna and quail (see Exod 16:4-15) and of the water from the rock (see Exod 17:4-7). What is often overlooked about both of these providential miracles is that they each were preceded by the people's grumbling and quarreling. It was not until after Yahweh had responded to their grumbling that the people were properly disposed to enter into a new covenant with Yahweh. And so, in chapter 19 of Exodus, we see the Israelites having traveled all the way to "the wilderness of Sinai." It is in the midst of that wilderness—in a new land filled with new challenges but also new beginnings—that a new covenant is established between Yahweh and the Israelites. And this covenant will mark the beginning of a new relationship between God and God's own people.

Each of the passages from Exodus will be considered separately. The questions that appear occasionally in the margins are for group discussion or personal reflection.

Understanding the Scenes Themselves

Exodus 16:1-3

[1]Having set out from Elim, the whole Israelite community came into the wilderness of Sin, which is between Elim and Sinai, on the fifteenth day of the second month after their departure from the land of Egypt. [2]Here in the wilderness the whole Israelite community grumbled against Moses and Aaron. [3]The Israelites said to them, "If only we had died at the LORD's hand in the land of Egypt, as we sat by our kettles of meat and ate our fill of bread! But you have led us into this wilderness to make this whole assembly die of famine!"

Notice first where the Israelites have traveled at this point. Far from the familiar (though unfree) confines of the pharaoh, they have now ventured south into the Sinai Peninsula, just to the west of the Gulf of Suez. The Scriptures tell us that they are in "the wilderness of Sin" (v. 1), which was somewhere between the towns of Elim and Sinai. And it was in this wilderness—perhaps both geographically and spiritually—that the people first began to complain.

But it was not just one or two people who grumbled. Rather, we are told that Moses and Aaron heard complaints from "the whole Israelite community" (v. 2), which apparently was united in its disdain for this new predicament in which they found themselves. Although no longer under the pharaoh's domain, they now also no longer knew where their next meal would

What are some characteristics of a physical wilderness that also apply to a spiritual wilderness?

come from. And so, they tell Moses and Aaron that back in Egypt at least they had "kettles of meat and ate our fill of bread!" (v. 3).

It is questionable at best whether the Israelites in fact would have had "kettles of meat" and their "fill of bread" as slaves in Egypt; certainly their treatment as slaves recorded in previous chapters would seem to dispute this possibility (see Exod 1:10-14). More likely, now that the Israelites have gained independence along with uncertainty, any trial or difficulty tends to make them look back with imagined and hyperbolic fondness on their days in Egypt—or, in more colloquial terms, the grass always seems greener on the other side. They are in uncharted territory, the newness of which makes them long for days that never really were as glorious as they now imagine them.

Exodus 17:1-3

[1]From the wilderness of Sin the whole Israelite community journeyed by stages, as the LORD directed, and encamped at Rephidim.

But there was no water for the people to drink, [2]and so they quarreled with Moses and said, "Give us water to drink." Moses replied to them, "Why do you quarrel with me? Why do you put the LORD to a test?" [3]Here, then, in their thirst for water, the people grumbled against Moses, saying, "Why then did you bring us up out of Egypt? To have us die of thirst with our children and our livestock?"

The Israelites' complaining and longing for the glory days of Egypt was rewarded in chapter 16 by Yahweh's intervention with quail and manna. Yet, the people would not be satisfied. In chapter 17, the Israelites venture out of the wilderness of Sin and into a new unfamiliar territory called Rephidim.

Whereas in chapter 16 they complained of hunger, here they complain of thirst. Again they are longing for the days in Egypt, where they at least had some idea of where to get a drink of water. Now, wandering about in the wilderness with no ready access to water and no idea from where their next drink might come, their uncertainty again gives way to quarreling and grumbling. And Yahweh again responds with great favor, by providing water from the rock struck by Moses.

Although the people's thirst may have been sated, their grumbling left its mark. The place in or near Rephidim was thereafter named "Massah and Meribah, because the Israelites quarreled there and tested the LORD, saying, 'Is the LORD in our midst or not?'" (Exod 17:7). Indeed, the very names of the place concretize the Israelites' grumbling: Massah is a derivation of the Hebrew word for "to test," and Meribah plays on the Hebrew root word for "to quarrel." Thus, the land itself is marked with a permanent reminder of people's penchant for testing, quarreling, and

What are some of the hungers and thirsts that most humans experience?

Do you have items that remind you of earlier times of uncertainty? Or even times of clarity?

grumbling with God whenever things seem most uncertain.

But while the people's quarreling may have hit a sore spot with Yahweh, it also drew them ever further into relationship with their God and with one another, setting the stage for the establishment of one of the more impactful covenants with the people of Israel.

Exodus 19:1-8

¹In the third month after the Israelites' departure from the land of Egypt, on the first day, they came to the wilderness of Sinai. ²After they made the journey from Rephidim and entered the wilderness of Sinai, they then pitched camp in the wilderness.

While Israel was encamped there in front of the mountain, ³Moses went up to the mountain of God. Then the Lord called to him from the mountain, saying: This is what you will say to the house of Jacob; tell the Israelites: ⁴You have seen how I treated the Egyptians and how I bore you up on eagles' wings and brought you to myself. ⁵Now, if you obey me completely and keep my covenant, you will be my treasured possession among all peoples, though all the earth is mine. ⁶You will be to me a kingdom of priests, a holy nation. That is what you must tell the Israelites." ⁷So Moses went and summoned the elders of the people. When he set before them all that the Lord had ordered him to tell them, ⁸all the people answered together, "Everything the Lord has said, we will do." Then Moses brought back to the Lord the response of the people.

Three months after they departed from Egypt—after their grumbling had been rewarded by Yahweh with quail, manna, and water from a rock—they traveled from Rephidim into the wilderness of Sinai. Note how the Israelites seem to be traveling from one wilderness to another: first in the wilderness of Sin (Exod 16), then into the wastelands of Rephidim (Exod 17), and now into the wilderness of Sinai (Exod 19:1-2). To drive home this theme of wilderness, the author uses the word "wilderness" three times in the first two verses of Exodus 19.

Can you recall times when it seemed the church or your family moved from one experience of wilderness to another?

It is in this continuing state of wilderness that the Israelites are presented with a decision point. Having seen all that Yahweh had done for them in the past (v. 4), they must now decide whether they will obey and keep Yahweh's covenant (v. 5). If they agree to that proposition, even though all the world belongs to Yahweh, they will be Yahweh's "treasured possession among all peoples, . . . a kingdom of priests, a holy nation" (vv. 5-6).

Note the threefold identity that will characterize the Israelites from here on out: (i) Yahweh's own treasured possession, (ii) a kingdom of priests, and (iii) a holy nation. Each of these three identities will be developed throughout the rest of the Old Testament (Lev 19:2; Deut 7:6; 14:2; 26:17-19; 32:8-9; Ps 135; Isa 61:6; Mal 3:17), as well as into the New Testament (Gal 3:29; 1 Pet 2:5-9; Rev 1:6; 5:9-10).

Note also the hierarchical progression of intermediaries through whom Yahweh's covenant plan is revealed. Yahweh first delivers this message to Moses from a mountain. Moses then takes Yahweh's proposal to the elders of the people (v. 7). Then, once everyone has digested what Yahweh is proposing through Moses, "all the people answered together," assenting to the covenant and promising to do everything the Lord is asking of them.

In many ways, the Sinai covenant in chapter 19 is the culmination and perfection of the partial revelations contained in chapter 16 (quail and manna) and chapter 17 (water from the rock). In the latter instances, the people received Yahweh's care and sustenance without actually having to give anything in return—they simply grumbled, complained, and murmured enough to provoke a loving response from a merciful God. But the Sinai covenant requires the Israelites to have some skin in the game. There is at least some progression out of their entitlement mind-set, in which they longed for the days of Egypt when the going got rough in unfamiliar territory. Now we see the people of Israel entering into a more bilateral relationship with Yahweh, which would seem to indicate that they are finally starting to embrace (rather than run away from) this new beginning of being the "people of Yahweh."

Praying the Word / Sacred Reading

The above three passages hinge on the Israel-ites' movement from a place of familiarity (Egypt) to a place of unfamiliarity (the wilderness). The exodus constitutes a new beginning for the people of Israel, but with that new beginning come many unknowns.

What areas of my life have been, or are now, places of wilderness in this journey of life? My wilderness may be physical (moving to a new town) but more often than not is spiritual or emotional.

- Where is God for me in the midst of my wilderness?

- Do I bring my complaints to God, trusting in his providential care?

- Am I ready to move away from simply demanding consolations from God (Exod 16 and 17) and toward consenting to God's divine will, trusting that God will make me part of his "treasured possession" (Exod 19)?

Let the words of these Scripture passages guide your meditation on your own wilderness journey and relationship with God. As you reflect on these passages, consider placing yourself in the scenes and seeing how you might react—in the midst of the grumbling and hungry crowd in the wilderness of Sin (Exod 16); among those quarreling for water at Rephidim (Exod 17); and finally in the wilderness of Sinai, when

Moses comes to tell the crowd about a new covenant being offered by Yahweh (Exod 19).

Living the Word

Consider ways to reach out to others who are going through their own "wilderness" or time of "new beginnings," for example,

- *new immigrants to your community;*

- *the homeless and hungry;*

- *expectant mothers in crisis pregnancy situations;*

- *those grieving the recent loss of a friend or loved one;*

- *those just starting their journey toward sobriety.*

Join, or offer to help start, a formal or informal support group that gives comfort and consolation to those going through these kinds of wildernesses. How can we respond to others' complaining and grumbling, while also leading them into the freedom that comes with giving themselves over to an intimate relationship with God?

New Hearts for New Beginnings

Begin by quietly asking God to assist you in your prayer and reflection. Then read Jeremiah 31:31-34, God's promise of a new covenant at the end of Israel's exile in Babylon.

Jeremiah 31:31-34

³¹See, days are coming—oracle of the LORD—when I will make a new covenant with the house of Israel and the house of Judah. ³²It will not be like the covenant I made with their ancestors the day I took them by the hand to lead them out of the land of Egypt. They broke my covenant, though I was their master—oracle of the LORD. ³³But this is the covenant I will make with the house of Israel after those days—oracle of the LORD. I will place my law within them, and write it upon their hearts; I will be their God, and they shall be my people. ³⁴They will no longer teach their friends and relatives, "Know the LORD!" Everyone, from least to greatest, shall know me—oracle of the LORD—for I will forgive their iniquity and no longer remember their sin.

*After reading and reflecting for a few moments
on the passage from Jeremiah, read the
background information in "Setting the Scene."*

Setting the Scene

Jeremiah is writing sometime around the year 626 BC, over six hundred years after the events described in Exodus. For the Israelites, much has changed, but much also remains the same. Having escaped enslavement by the pharaoh in Egypt, they are now residing in Israel. Another superpower, the Assyrian Empire, falls, and they find themselves under the dominating reign of the Babylonian Empire. In fact, political wars and tensions between the larger powers of Egypt, the Assyrians, and the Babylonians eventually result in the Babylonians seizing Jerusalem around 588 BC and destroying it and its temple the following year, leading to the Babylonian captivity or exile. Jeremiah's prophetic writings preceded the exile of the Israelites and are clearly colored by the preexilic tensions. He speaks to the struggles that the exiles would endure. However, Jeremiah's writings also look forward prophetically to a grander plan that Yahweh has in mind for his chosen people.

Consider a time when some event or series of events shook you out of complacency. What finally helped you to move forward or to let go?

The prophecy in chapter 31 appears a little over halfway through the book of Jeremiah. Leading up to chapter 31 is a series of oracles about the previous kings and leaders of Judah (chapters 1–22); warnings about evil shepherds and false prophets (chapters 23 and 27–28); prophesies about those who bear bad fruit and the coming period of exile (chapters 24–25); and finally, prophesies about the restoration of the Israelite people and their return home to the Promised Land (chapters 30–31).

In many ways this section of chapter 31 functions as the apex of the entire book of Jeremiah. The Israelites had long ago reached the Promised Land, but they were about to be exiled because of their misplaced trust in failed kings and false prophets. Jeremiah is trying to prepare the Israelites not only for the trials ahead but also for the new covenant that Yahweh will establish with them. And this new covenant will mark a new beginning in how they relate to God.

> *The passage from Jeremiah will now be examined a few verses at a time to allow for deeper understanding. Questions in the margin are for personal use or group discussion.*

Understanding the Scene Itself

³¹**See, days are coming—oracle of the LORD— when I will make a new covenant with the house of Israel and the house of Judah. ³²It will not be like the covenant I made with their ancestors the day I took them by the hand to lead them out of the land of Egypt. They broke my covenant, though I was their master—oracle of the LORD.**

At the very beginning of this prophecy, we read language that would have stood out to the Israelites: "new covenant." This is the first and only time this phrase is used in the Old

Testament. As Christians, we tend to view everything in the Old Testament as prefiguring the New, but such a reading would not have occurred to the Israelites who were bearing the brunt of Jeremiah's prophetic words.

Jeremiah's words were intended not necessarily as predictions about the future, but as words of comfort and consolation to the Israelites in the midst of their upcoming exile to Babylon. They would no doubt feel abandoned by their God who had previously rescued them from slavery and made them his own. And so, Jeremiah enters the picture as a vehicle of God's promise of continued providential care.

Foreseeing that the Israelites might equate this new covenant as just another update to the one at Sinai (see Exod 19:1-8), Jeremiah dispels that notion in verse 32, saying that this will not be like the covenant established with the Israelites after they were led out of Egypt. Their ancestors broke that covenant, rendering it ineffective.

We see examples of Yahweh's anger and disappointment over the broken covenants throughout the Old Testament but also in earlier chapters of Jeremiah. For example, chapter 2 contains a lengthy recounting by Yahweh of all the ways in which the Israelites were unfaithful to him and the prior covenants, even going so far as to worship the god Baal and other false idols (Jer 2:8). And in chapter 7, Yahweh laments that he did not demand from the Israelites sacrifices or burnt offerings, but only that they listen to his voice and obey his commands—yet "they did not listen to me, nor did they pay attention" (Jer 7:24).

> Has there ever been a time when someone helped to remind you of God's care and plan for you? What do you recall from that experience?

Indeed, says Yahweh, from the very day of their liberation from the Egyptians, the Israelites repeatedly refused to listen to him (Jer 7:25-26).

What practices help you to truly listen to God?

The Israelites' failure to listen to Yahweh's commands prompts him to create a covenant that is *internal* to their very being, such that there will no longer be any excuse not to hear the voice of the Lord.

³³**But this is the covenant I will make with the house of Israel after those days—oracle of the L**ORD**. I will place my law within them, and write it upon their hearts; I will be their God, and they shall be my people. ³⁴They will no longer teach their friends and relatives, "Know the L**ORD**!" Everyone, from least to greatest, shall know me—oracle of the L**ORD**—for I will forgive their iniquity and no longer remember their sin.**

Rather than writing on stone tablets like the covenant at Sinai, Yahweh will write this new covenant "upon their hearts" (v. 33). For the Israelites, the Law was sacred, and compliance with the Law resulted in right relationship with God. In order to follow the Law, it had to be handed down and taught from one generation to the next. But in verse 33, Jeremiah is foretelling a new kind of covenant that will no longer be *external*, but *internal*—placed on their very hearts.

As the scholar Walter Brueggemann has noted, it may be that this covenant is in continuity with prior covenants, but the method of communicating it has now drastically changed. Yahweh is moving away from a strictly externally based set of rules and regulations and toward an internally placed knowledge of God, which motivates more out of love than mere obligation.

One result of this *internal* reordering of God's covenant is the method of its transmission. You may recall that with the Sinai covenant, there is a distinctive hierarchical order to Yahweh's self-revelation and how that was communicated to the people: first to Moses, then to the elders, then to all the people, and then back to Yahweh through Moses (Exod 19:6-8). But, with the new internal covenant prophesied by Jeremiah, the religious leaders "will no longer teach their friends and relatives," because everyone "from least to greatest" will know the Lord (v. 34). This new covenant thus becomes more personalized, more intimate, and less dependent on external experts for validation.

Another result of the *internal* reordering is that, unlike the bilateral covenant in Exodus that required the people's assent, the covenant in Jeremiah is distinctly unilateral. The Israelites in Exodus promised to obey and thus could break the covenant by failing to do so. In Jeremiah, however, the covenant is not contingent on the people's listening or obeying, because it is now written on their very hearts.

Everyone "from least to greatest" will know the Lord.

–Jer 31:34

Finally, the new covenant carries with it a unique healing characteristic: forgiveness of the people's iniquities and forgetting all their sins (v. 34). Whereas the previous covenants were contingent on the people's faithfulness, in many ways this new covenant will become unbreakable. The people of God will know God in their very hearts. And the people's transgressions will be not only forgiven but completely forgotten—making this new covenant entirely of God's own initiative.

What typically prevents you from embracing God's forgiveness?

Jeremiah's prophetic vision of a new kind of covenant is later reiterated by another prophet, Ezekiel. Ezekiel uses almost identical language, but with an even more visceral emphasis on the reordering of the human condition as a result of this new covenantal relationship to come:

> I will give them another heart and a new spirit I will put within them. From their bodies I will remove the hearts of stone, and give them hearts of flesh, so that they walk according to my statutes, taking care to keep my ordinances. Thus they will be my people, and I will be their God. (Ezek 11:19-20)

Whereas Jeremiah sees this new covenant as being written on the people's hearts, Ezekiel goes a step further: the people's stony hearts will be removed from them entirely, and God will place a new heart and a new spirit within them.

Although Jeremiah and Ezekiel did not have the benefit of foreseeing the incarnation, it is nearly impossible for Christians to read these sections without viewing them at least in part

In a general way, the covenant refers to the relationship between God and his people. In what ways do you see God always renewing this covenant?

as prophecies of the coming of Jesus Christ. Indeed, Jesus' statement in Luke 22:20 would seem to be a fulfillment of the new covenant prophesied by Jeremiah, when Jesus says at the Last Supper: "This cup is the new covenant in my blood." Various other New Testament authors also pick up on the themes of this Jeremiah passage (e.g., 1 Cor 11:25; 2 Cor 3:5-14). And the Jeremiah passage is quoted in its entirety in the book of Hebrews (8:8-12), making it the longest direct quote of an Old Testament passage within the New Testament.

Notwithstanding the implications of God becoming human in the person of Jesus, it must have come as a shock to the Israelites to be told that Yahweh would be establishing a "new covenant," which would be written on their very hearts. For generations, this people of the Law had focused on learning, understanding, and then teaching the written text of the Law as the sole means of coming into relationship with the Lord.

Now, after generations of doing things one way, they were being prepared to do them another.

To say this "new covenant" would have stretched them out of their comfort zone would be an understatement. But there's no overstating the importance of going outside one's comfort zone in order to truly encounter the living God.

Praying the Word / Sacred Reading

Read back slowly through the passages from Jeremiah as well as Ezekiel. Spend time particularly on Jeremiah 31:33-34 and Ezekiel 11:19.

Prayerfully consider the following questions as you read through those lines:

- Has my relationship with the Lord become too routine, such that I tend to take it for granted?

- Is my relationship with God based primarily on fulfilling a certain "to-do list" of prayers or religious observances, or do I experience God deep within my very being?

- Have I become too content to rest in my comfort zone, where I expect God to be, or am I open to new ways in which God might speak to me?

- How might God be preparing me for a new heart and a new spirit?

- Am I willing to go outside my comfort zone for the kind of relationship with God that he so fervently desires to have with me?

Living the Word

Consider sharing your faith with someone who feels ostracized, marginalized, or exiled (like the Israelites to whom Jeremiah was writing). Like Jeremiah, let your faith-sharing be focused not on a set of rules or regulations, but on how God has personally touched and written on your very heart.

With this new covenant prophesied by Jeremiah, God not only forgives all our sins but even forgets them. Are there people in your life whom you struggle to forgive? Maybe circumstances are such that complete reconciliation at this point seems impossible. If there appears to be no way forward toward forgiveness and reconciliation, consider praying for that person and his/her own special intentions—sometimes, praying for those who have wronged us is the best way to achieve the inner peace that comes with forgiveness and letting go, even if reconciliation seems unlikely.

Opening Our Hearts to New Callings

After inviting God to assist you in your prayer and study, read the following passage from the Gospel of Matthew, which describes the new beginning experienced by one of Jesus' followers.

Matthew 9:9-13

[9]As Jesus passed on from there, he saw a man named Matthew sitting at the customs post. He said to him, "Follow me." And he got up and followed him. [10]While he was at table in his house, many tax collectors and sinners came and sat with Jesus and his disciples. [11]The Pharisees saw this and said to his disciples, "Why does your teacher eat with tax collectors and sinners?" [12]He heard this and said, "Those who are well do not need a physician, but the sick do. [13]Go and learn the meaning of the words, 'I desire mercy, not sacrifice.' I did not come to call the righteous but sinners."

Setting the Scene

In the first chapter of this book, we reflected on God calling the Israelites out of wandering in the wilderness and into a covenant relationship with him (Exod 16–19). In the second chapter, we considered breaking free from preconceived notions of how God wants to relate to us, and opening our hearts to letting God write upon them a new covenant (Jer 31). In this final chapter, our Scripture study and reflection become more personal. What does it mean not just to follow a set of religious rules and regulations but to have a real, personal, intimate encounter with the new and everlasting covenant himself, Jesus Christ?

The Gospel of Matthew is one of the most important texts in all of Christianity. Its placement at the very beginning of the New Testament demonstrates its significance in early Christianity and the traditional belief that it was the first gospel written (although most scholars now believe Mark's gospel may have been composed first). Besides its obvious divine inspiration, it is also a masterpiece of literary storytelling, weaving together Old Testament prophecies with their fulfillment in the coming of the Christ. And the stories in this gospel tend to emphasize the personal, intimate encounters that Jesus had with others. So, it should be no surprise that this gospel includes a story of the conversion of its namesake, Matthew.

The story of the conversion of Matthew appears in chapter 9. Leading up to that, we read through the genealogy and infancy narratives of Jesus and then several chapters of his preaching of the coming of the kingdom of God—chapters that include the Beatitudes, the Lord's Prayer, various moral teachings, and accounts of multiple healings. It is no coincidence that the dramatic and out-of-the-blue calling of Matthew—who was a notorious sinner in need of healing himself—is sandwiched between multiple healing stories within chapter 9.

The passage from Matthew will now be examined a few verses at a time to allow for deeper understanding. Questions in the margin continue to encourage reflection or discussion.

Understanding the Scene Itself

⁹**As Jesus passed on from there, he saw a man named Matthew sitting at the customs post. He said to him, "Follow me." And he got up and followed him. ¹⁰While he was at table in his house, many tax collectors and sinners came and sat with Jesus and his disciples.**

At the beginning of this passage, in verse 9, we read that Jesus had just "passed on" from healing a paralytic in the midst of a crowd in Capernaum. Capernaum was at a crossroads of commerce that traveled between Egypt and

Damascus, and so there were plenty of items in transit to be taxed. It was also in the territory that fell under Herod's jurisdiction, so it is probable that Matthew was working to collect taxes directly for Herod, who in turn reported to and supported Caesar and the Roman Empire.

Presumably, Jesus is still traveling through Capernaum when he comes upon a customs post at which Matthew is sitting. The action happens fast. Jesus sees Matthew; Jesus says, "Follow me"; and Matthew "got up and followed him." How does one explain what may be the quickest conversion story in all of Scripture?

Imagine Jesus saying, "Follow me" to you at this time in your life. What might be holding you back? Why would you follow him?

At least some scholars attribute Matthew's quick lifestyle change to the constraints of the oral tradition on which this written gospel must have been based—i.e., there must have been more to the story of Matthew's conversion than this quick interlude, but due to oral tradition not all of those dynamics were retained. But such an attempt to explain away the abruptness of Matthew's conversion strikes this author as too convenient. The gospels are replete with more complete dialogues between Jesus and his converts—so why would Matthew's conversion story not be capable of retaining similar details? Indeed, perhaps it is the abruptness of his conversion that Matthew wants us to ponder.

Verse 10 contains an interesting ambiguity, as it states that "he was at table in his house" but does not state whose house it is (although Luke 5:29 has the banquet occurring at Matthew's house). However, one thing that is not ambiguous is the correlation between sinners and  tax collectors, who were viewed as conspiratorially aligned with the Roman authorities and who often extorted money from the people for their own selfish gain. It would not have struck the audience as odd to group "tax collectors" with "sinners," as tax collectors were notorious for extorting money from people who had no idea how much they actually owed in taxes. And so, we see Jesus dining with sinners.

¹¹The Pharisees saw this and said to his disciples, "Why does your teacher eat with tax collectors and sinners?" ¹²He heard this and said, "Those who are well do not need a physician, but the sick do. ¹³Go and learn the meaning of the words, 'I desire mercy, not sacrifice.' I did not come to call the righteous but sinners."

The Pharisees do what they do best: question Jesus' actions. But notice that they pose their questions to Jesus' disciples, not to him directly (v. 11). Perhaps they didn't want to cause a scene, or perhaps they simply weren't brave enough to direct their questions to Jesus' face. Either way, their passive-aggressive approach was indicative of their desire to undermine the following that Jesus had begun to amass. But instead of pretending like he did not hear the criticism, Jesus immediately speaks up to defend not only his disciples but also his own practices.

Matthew depicts Jesus as a teacher and healer. Do these descriptions relate to your experience of Jesus? What else might you add?

Jesus responds with a proverb that would have been familiar to Greek thought: "Those who are well do not need a physician, but the sick do" (v. 12). In the verse prior, the Pharisees had referred to Jesus as a "teacher." In Greek thought, philosophers were considered to be "doctors of the soul." And so Jesus makes a play on these two concepts, combining them into one. He does not scoff at being called merely "teacher." Rather, he embraces that role but then transforms it into something much bigger. He is not merely a teacher but a physician—and like the great Greek philosophers who were physicians of the soul, he has come to heal those whose souls are sick, like tax collectors and sinners.

The final verse of this paragraph contains language very much in line with the priorities of Pope Francis. Jesus instructs the Pharisees to go

Pope Francis has stated, "The works of mercy are 'handcrafted,' in the sense that none of them is alike. Our hands can craft them in a thousand different ways, and even though the one God inspires them, and they are all fashioned from the same 'material,' mercy itself, each one takes on a different form" (*Misericordia et Misera*, 20).

and learn the meaning of the phrase "I desire mercy, not sacrifice" (v. 13). This is another phrase with which his audience would have been familiar (this time owing to their Jewish faith), as Jesus is referencing Hosea 6:6. For Jews, this phrase from Hosea would become particularly important after the destruction of the temple in Jerusalem around AD 70, as they could no longer offer up the required sacrifices. For early Christians, however, this line would take on new meaning.

Name some of the various ways you see God's mercy at work in the world.

Jesus' sacrifice on the cross is the final, eternal sacrifice that reconciles humankind with the Father. Jesus' great commission at the end of the Gospel of Matthew is for his disciples to go and teach all nations, forming new disciples to go on mission. This missionary discipleship is not about offering up individual sacrifices or a myopic focus on one's own individual relationship with God. Nor is missionary discipleship about cordoning oneself off from any interaction with those who are in need of healing (e.g., sinners), out of fear of losing one's own holiness in the process.

Rather, following Jesus' command in Matthew 9:13, the Christian is called to be a missionary of mercy, especially to sinners, the outcasts, and the marginalized. And a Christian must avoid the temptation to fall into the mind-set of the Pharisee,

How has your
own discipleship
grown as you
reach beyond
what is familiar
or comfortable?

in which we are so afraid of becoming tainted by others' sinfulness that we refuse to interact with anyone other than those whom we deem "pure enough" for us to befriend.

It is from within this very group—sinners, outcasts, marginalized—that Jesus quite literally plucks out Matthew somewhat spontaneously. Jesus' calling of Matthew demonstrates that our God is a God of surprises. Even when we feel most ostracized from God, God takes the initiative to reach into that place of ostracism, point to us and look us in the eyes, and say, "Follow me." Jesus does not lead with argument or debate. He does not even attempt to enter into dialogue with Matthew. Instead, Jesus has built a reputation around town healing those who are sick and infirmed, and he goes to Matthew (who is sick in spirit) and calls him out of that desolation.

It is almost impossible to imagine the kind of new beginning that all this must have entailed for Matthew. One minute he was gathered around a table full of money inside a customs post, presumably surrounded by fellow money counters and tax collectors. The next minute, he has left behind his livelihood, his money, and his comfort zone, all to follow someone whom he had literally just encountered in person for the first time.

Such a radical turnaround speaks to the immense draw that one confronts when faced with the person of Jesus Christ. But it also speaks to Matthew's apparent openness to being drawn into a new relationship with God, a new way of living life. In the book of Exodus, the Israelites were called into a new covenant with Yahweh. In Jeremiah, Yahweh planned to create a new covenant that would be written on people's very hearts. In Matthew, we see a sinful man who personally encounters that new covenant himself, Jesus Christ.

It is the personification of the new covenant that makes Matthew's spontaneous conversion a possibility. A covenant written on stone tablets or in special books cannot so quickly convert. But a covenant in the form of a person—the person of Jesus—has the power to write itself on our very hearts and change our lives in an instant . . . if we remain open to that possibility. Matthew could not have known what his future would hold when he suddenly decided to leave behind his tax collecting and trade it in for the unknown of discipleship with Jesus. But Matthew knew what so many of us fail to grasp: each person's future is filled with uncertainty; the only certainty is that our unknown futures are better off placed in God's hands than tightly grasped in our own.

Have you ever experienced God's presence with you in the midst of the unknown? What grace can you recall?

Praying the Word / Sacred Reading

As with the prayer over the stories in Exodus, you might try closing your eyes, quieting your mind, and imagining yourself in this scene from Matthew 9. As you imagine this bustling town filled with economic activity, envision being in the customs post where money is counted and goods are taxed. Imagine that you are Matthew, or one of the other tax collectors. There is no electricity, and so the room is lit solely by natural light, perhaps not very well.

Imagine what lies on the table in front of you. For Matthew, it was money, maybe some goods awaiting taxation, maybe tools for measuring and weighing items—all worldly things that kept him connected to this place of darkness, of sinfulness, of selfish gains, of attachment to things of this world. But for you, what is on your table? What parts of your life are you holding on to rather than surrendering to God? What parts are enslaving you, haunting you, or bringing you down? Imagine that all those things are on that table in front of you, and sense the attachment you feel to them.

Then, imagine that Jesus walks in the door unexpectedly. With his entrance comes new, fresh light into this dreary place. He does not judge. He does not condemn. He does not even try to convince you with intellectual arguments about how all those things on the table really aren't doing you any good. Instead, he simply looks you in the eyes, maybe reaches his hand out toward you, calls you by name, and says: "Follow me."

How do you respond? What are you still tempted to cling to? Does this new beginning in Jesus Christ bring you excitement, joy, anxiety, trepidation? Whatever it is, share all that with Jesus as you begin following him out of that room, through the town, and into a future that he alone holds in his hands.

Living the Word

In this passage of Matthew's gospel, we clearly see that Jesus is not afraid to dine with sinners and tax collectors—those whom the Jewish leaders would have considered to be impure and unclean. And, in fact, Jesus commissions each disciple to go into the world and do the same.

Consider going outside your comfort zone and forming relationships with people at the margins of society. Everyone has their own "society"—it may be in your parish, your family, your group of friends, your neighborhood, or your workplace. And in every society there are people "at the margins." Research what ministries or agencies in your area might help you make these connections with the poor, the sick, or those neglected in some way. Jesus calls each of us to reach out to those persons, without any fear that in doing so we ourselves might become unclean. Jesus has lit up our world. We are now called to bring the light of Jesus into the darkest places of our lives and of the lives of others.